English Code 1

Workbook

Progress Chart

You did it!	Great job!	Fantastic!	Super!

Unit 8

Unit 7

Unit 6

Unit 5

Unit 4

Unit 3

Unit 2

Unit 1

Creativity   Critical thinking   Coding   Communication

Contents

Welcome!

 How can I have fun at school?

1 002 Listen and number. Then write.

bag   book   chair   door   pencil   table   window

_____   _____   _____   _____

_____   _____   _____

2 Cover a photo in 1. Play *What's missing?*

Book!

Yes!

3 003 Listen to the song. Then greet your partner.

Hello, how are you?

I'm OK, thanks.

How about you?

I'm great, thank you.

My colorful classroom

VOCABULARY

I will learn color words and number words **1-10**.

1 004 **Listen and complete in the correct color.**

1 ___ed   2 ___ink   3 ___reen   4 ___range   5 ___lack

6 ___urple   7 ___rown   8 ___lue   9 ___ellow

2 Look and color. Then say the colors and numbers.

3 Look at 2. Which numbers from 0–10 are missing?

MATH ZONE

4 Read and draw.

7 purple books

4 pink chairs

I can use color words and number words 1–10.

5

Language lab

GRAMMAR: OPEN YOUR BOOK

I will learn how to follow instructions in English.

1 005 **Listen and continue the sequence.**

CODE CRACKER

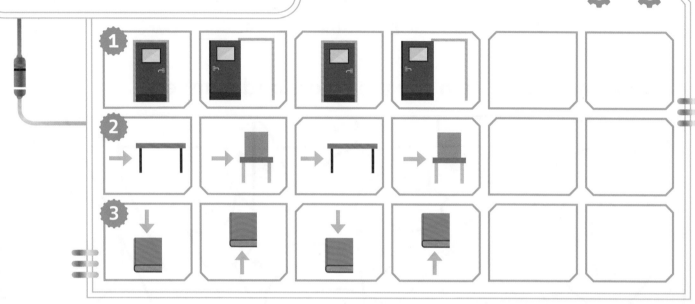

2 Read and match.

1 Open your book.

2 Pick up your pencil.

3 Stand up.

4 Open the window.

5 Pick up your bag.

● Put down your pencil.

● Put down your bag.

● Shut your book.

● Sit down.

● Shut the window.

3 **Play *Opposites tennis*.**

Open the door!

Shut the door!

I can follow instructions in English.

Story lab

Hello!

1 **Read the story again. Then complete.**

1 Hi! I'm _____ . I'm _____ .

Hello! My name is _____ .
I'm _____ .

2 Here's _____ ! She's _____ .

Hello!

2 **Read and match. Then ask and answer.**

8 •
4 •
9 •
2 •

● N-I-N-E

● E-I-G-H-T

● T-W-O

● F-O-U-R

How do you spell 8?

E-I-G-H-T

3 **Order and write the questions. Then ask and answer.**

1 you? are How   _____

2 What's name? your   _____

3 do How spell that? you   _____

4 old you? How are   _____

I can read a story and learn how to introduce myself.

1 Let's play!

How can I make a toy that floats?

1 🎧 006 **Listen to the song and number.**

CODE CRACKER

2 💡 **Circle and say. Then check ☑ what is missing from the song.**

1 ☐ airplane / train

2 ☐ car / boat

3 ☐ airplane / boat

4 ☐ train / car

Go airplane!

3 **Which car gets to school first? Count the blocks and circle.**

MATH ZONE

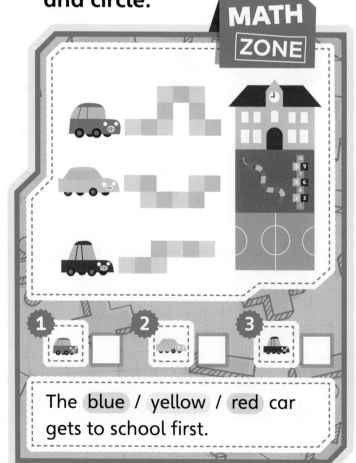

1 ☐ **2** ☐ **3** ☐

The blue / yellow / red car gets to school first.

Toy room

VOCABULARY

I will learn toy words.

1 Find and circle 10 toys.

buscardollballtrainoctopusairplanebuildingblocksboatteddybear

2 Look and write.

1

2

3

4

5

_____ _____ _____ _____ _____

6

7

8

EXTRA VOCABULARY

_____ _____ _____

3 🎧 007 Read, listen, and check ☑. Then color.

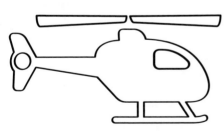

a red helicopter ☐

a blue car ☐

a green van ☐

a red airplane ☐

a blue motorbike ☐

a green bus ☐

I can use toy words.

9

Language lab 1

GRAMMAR 1: IT'S A / AN ...

I will name toy words using **It's a / It's an.**

1 Read and match.

1 I am   2 It is   3 What is   4 He is   5 She is

What's   It's   He's   She's   I'm

2 Look and complete.

1 What's this?

It's _a teddy bear_ .

2 What's this?

It's _____ ball.

3 What's this?

_____ an airplane.

4 What's this?

_____ doll.

5 What's this?

It's _____ .

3 Make a toy silhouette. Then ask and answer.

What's this?

It's a doll.

I can name toy words using It's a / It's an ... .

Story lab

READING

I will read a story about toys.

Let's play together

1 ⚙ Make your story book. ➡ page 97

1 Order and write the page numbers.

2 Complete the story.

3 Draw a cover.

4 Complete the story review.

2 Look and complete.

1 What's this?

It's _____ .

2 What's this?

It's _____ .

3 What's this?

It's _____ .

3 ⚙ Make a toy from a box. Then ask and answer.

 What's this?

 It's a car.

I can read a story about toys.

Phonics lab

P AND B

1 Look, listen, and circle p or b. Then say.

Color me !

1

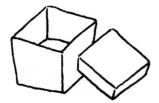

p
b ox

2

p
b ed

3

p
b en

4

p
b anda

2 Write the missing letters. Then say.

The _____anda has a _____en and a _____encil.

3 Listen and write the missing letters. Then read and color.

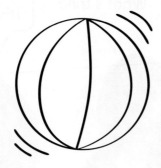

1 What's this?
It's a _____lue _____all.

2 What's this?
It's a _____urple _____arrot.

I can use the **p** and **b** sounds.

12

Experiment lab

ENGINEERING: MATERIALS

I will learn about toy materials.

1 Look and write.

> fabric   metal
> plastic   wood

1   It's an _____ .
    It's made of _____ .

2   It's a _____ _____ .
    It's made of _____ .

3   It's a _____ .
    It's made of _____ .

4   It's a _____ .
    It's made of _____ .

EXPERIMENT TIME

Report

1 Complete the chart.

Toy	Material	Float	Sink

2 Write your report.

Float or sink?

It's a boat. It's made of plastic. It floats.

Float or sink?

It's _____ . It's made of
_____ . It _____ .

I know about toy materials.

Language lab 2

GRAMMAR 2: IT'S A BIG / SMALL …

I will describe toys.

1 Look, read, and number.

1   It's a black building block.

2   It's a small building block.

3   It's a blue building block.

4   It's a big building block.

2 Order and write. Then look and write T (True) or F (False).

CODE CRACKER

1   big   It's   bear.   teddy   a

_____

2   ball.   It's   big   a

_____

3   a   car.   small   It's

_____

4   red   a   It's   airplane.

_____

3 Look at 2. Correct the false sentences.

1   _____   2   _____

I can describe toys.

I know!

I will ask and answer about objects.

I don't know.

1 Listen and say
I know or I don't know.

2 Look, listen, and check ☑.

3 Ask and answer. Then complete.

What's this?

I don't know.

I know! It's an airplane.

It's _____ .   It's _____ .   It's _____ .

I can ask and answer about objects.

Make a toy that floats

Project report

1 Check ☑ for your toy.

Type of toy				
bus ☐	car ☐	airplane ☐	boat ☐	train ☐
doll ☐	ball ☐	teddy bear ☐	octopus ☐	
building blocks ☐	_____ ☐			

Size	Material	
big ☐ small ☐	paper ☐	metal ☐
Float or sink?	fabric ☐	plastic ☐
float ☐ sink ☐	wood ☐	

2 Complete your project report.

My toy boat

It's a paper boat.
It's orange.
It's small.
It floats!

My toy _____
It's a _____ .
It's _____ .
It's big / small.
It floats / sinks.

I can make a toy that floats.

3 💬 Present your report to your family and friends.

This is my toy boat. It's made of paper.

4 Read, look, and number.

1 It's made of fabric.

2 It's made of wood.

3 It's a big toy.

4 It's a small toy.

5 It floats.

6 It sinks.

What's this?

It's a small train.

5 💬 Look at 4. Ask and answer.

6 💡 Read and write. Then complete a clue for your partner.

It's small.
It's plastic.
It's red.
It's _____ .

It's _____ .
It's _____ .
It's _____ .
It's a/an _____ .

Now go to your Progress Chart on page 2.

2 Art Club!

How can I make an art store?

1 🎧 012 **Listen to the song and color in order.**

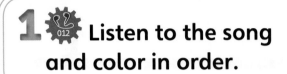

2 Read and write the numbers.

MATH ZONE

1 four red crayons + two blue crayons

$\boxed{4}$ + $\boxed{2}$ =

$\boxed{6}$ crayons

2 two green markers + one pink marker

$\boxed{}$ + $\boxed{}$ =

$\boxed{}$ markers

3 five orange coloring pencils + three yellow coloring pencils

$\boxed{}$ + $\boxed{}$ =

$\boxed{}$ coloring pencils

3 💡 **Match, write, and say.**

_____

_____

_____

Red crayon!

What do we need?

VOCABULARY

I will learn art item words.

1 Write the words.

1 p c e o n l c o i r l i s n h g a p r e p n e c n i e l r

   <u>pencil sharpener</u>   <u>coloring pencil</u>

2 m c a r r a k y e o r n

   _____   _____

3 p p e a n i c n i t l b c r a u s s e h

_____   _____

2 Look and write.

EXTRA VOCABULARY

3 013 Look, listen, and match. Then ask and answer.

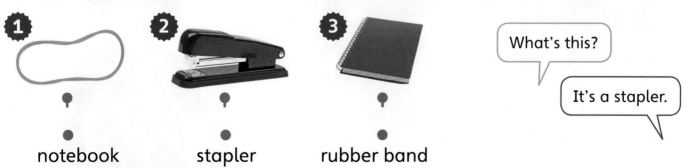

notebook   stapler   rubber band

What's this?

It's a stapler.

I can use art item words.

Language lab 1

GRAMMAR 1: THERE'S / ARE ...

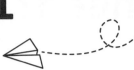

*I will learn to count using **There's / There are**.*

1 Read and circle.

1 There's / There are two markers.

2 There's / There are a paint pot.

3 There's / There are a pencil case.

4 There's / There are four glue sticks.

2 Look and complete. Then write T (True) or F (False).

1 ___There are___ ten markers ___T___

2 _____ three rulers. ___

3 _____ one coloring pencil. ___

4 _____ a paint pot. ___

5 _____ nine crayons. ___

6 _____ an eraser. ___

7 _____ a pencil sharpener. ___

8 _____ three glue sticks. ___

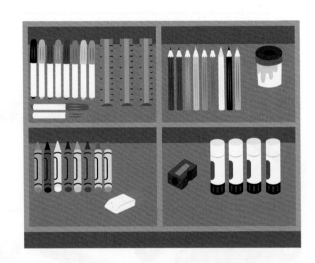

3 Count the items in your pencil case. Then tell your partner.

There are four markers.

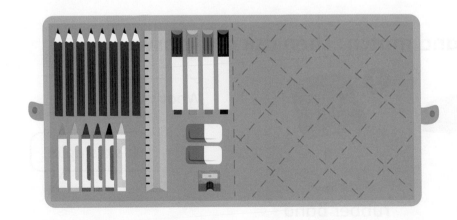

I can count art items using There's / There are .

Story lab

READING

I will read a story about the play house.

A rainbow play house

1 Make your story book. → page 99

1 Order and write the page numbers.

2 Complete the story.

3 Draw a cover.

4 Complete the story review.

2 Look and complete.

1 There's blue, yellow, and _____ paint.

2 There's orange, blue, and _____ paint.

3 There's blue, red, and _____ paint.

3 Design your own play house. Then say.

There's a small table.

I can read a story about the play house.

I will learn the **d** and **t** sounds.

1 014 **Look, listen, and circle d or t. Then say.**

1 The | d / t | uck talks to the | d / t | iger.

2 The | d / t | urtle is named | D / T | aisy.

2 Write d or t. Then say.

Color me!

1 ____able   2 ____oor   3 ____en

3 015 **Listen and write the missing letters. Then read and draw.**

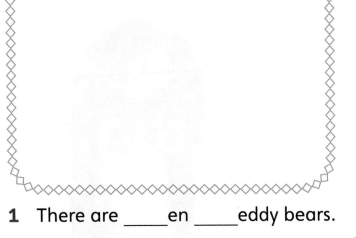

1 There are ____en ____eddy bears.   2 There's a ____og and a ____oll.

 I can use the **d** and **t** sounds.

Experiment lab

ART AND DESIGN: MIXING COLORS

I will learn about mixing colors.

1 Look and label. Then circle *P* for *primary colors* or *S* for *secondary colors*.

blue   green   orange
purple   red   yellow

1 _____
   P / S

2 _____
   P / S

3 _____
   P / S

4 _____
   P / S

5 _____
   P / S

6 _____
   P / S

EXPERIMENT TIME

Report

1 Complete the chart.

Color 1	Color 2	Result

2 Write your report.

Dark and light colors

red + white = pink

It's a light color.

How can I make dark and light colors?

red + white = _____
It's a light / dark color.

red + green = _____
It's a light / dark color.

black + white = _____
It's a light / dark color.

I know about mixing colors.

23

Language lab 2

GRAMMAR 2: HOW MANY ...?

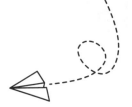

I will ask about art items using How many.

1 Read and match.

1 How many erasers are there? •

2 How many paint pots are there? •

3 How many pencil cases are there? •

• There are three paint pots.

• There's one pencil case.

• There are five erasers.

2 Order and write. Then complete.

CODE CRACKER

1 there?　paint　How　are　pots　many

_____

There are _____ paint pots.

2 many　there?　How　are　markers

_____

There _____ markers.

3 sharpeners　How　pencil　there?　are　many

_____

_____ pencil sharpener.

3 ✹ Guess the number of building blocks. Then check with your partner.

How many yellow building blocks are there?

There are seven yellow building blocks.

MATH ZONE

 **I can** ask about art items using How many ...?

Being polite

COMMUNICATION

I will ask and answer politely.

1 🎧 016 Listen and number. Then say.

Thank you. ☐

Here you go. ☐

Two paintbrushes, please. ☐

2 🎧 017 Listen and draw 🙂 or 🙁.

1

◯

2

◯

3

◯

3 💬 Role-play a toy store.

Two balls, please.

Here you go.

Thank you.

I can ask and answer about items politely.

PROJECT AND REVIEW UNIT 2

Make an art store

Project report

1 Complete for your art store.

Art item	Number
rulers	
markers	
coloring pencils	
crayons	
paint pots	
glue sticks	
erasers	
pencil sharpeners	
paintbrushes	
pencil cases	

2 Complete your project report.

My art store

There are four markers.
There are five rulers.
There are seven erasers.
There's one pencil case.

My art store

There's / There are _____.
There's / There are _____.
There's / There are _____.
There's / There are _____.

26

I can make an art store.

3 🗨 **Present your report to your family and friends.**

> This is my art store. There are four markers.

4 Count and write.

coloring pencils ☐

paint pots ☐

glue sticks ☐

crayons ☐

erasers ☐

markers ☐

5 🗨 **Look at 4. Ask and answer.**

> How many rulers are there?

> There are three rulers.

6 💡 **Read and circle. Then complete.**

Primary / Secondary colors	Primary / Secondary colors
_____ three blue rulers.	There's one green _____.
There's one red _____.	There are two _____ markers.
There are _____ yellow erasers.	_____ one orange pencil sharpener.

Now go to your Progress Chart on page 2.

1 Checkpoint

1 Read and match.

1 pencil	2 teddy	3 paint	4 building	5 glue
•	•	•	•	•
•	•	•	•	•
bear	blocks	stick	sharpener	pot

2 Draw a path and color.

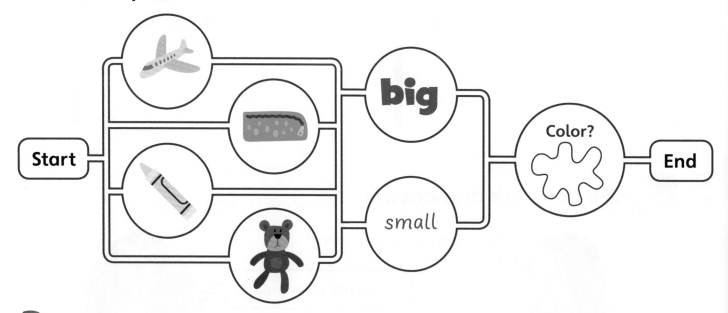

Start   big   small   Color?   End

3 Look at 2. Complete and draw.

1   What's this?   It's (a / an) _____ .

2   Is it big or small?   It's _____ .

3   What color is it?   It's _____ .

4   How many _____ are there in your class?

    There (is / are) _____ _____ .

Craft around the world

CULTURE

1 Look, read, and circle.

1 It's a bag / book .

2 It's an airplane / octopus .

3 It's a bus / car .

4 It's a llama / teddy bear .

2 Look at 1. Ask and answer.

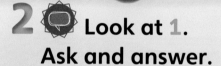

What's this?

It's origami! It's a book.

3 Count, circle, and write. Then check with your partner.

> airplane   dolls   glue stick   paintbrushes   paint pots   rulers

1 There's / There are eight _____ .

2 There's / There are nine _____ .

3 There's / There are four _____ .

4 There's / There are one _____ .

5 There's / There are two _____ .

6 There's / There are one _____ .

How many dolls are there?

There are eight dolls.

3 Families

How can I make a family decoration?

1 🎧 018 **Listen to the song. Choose and write words to make a new chorus.**

> **1** dad   mom   baby
>
> **2** happy   small   great

CODE CRACKER

There's **1** _____ and me,

1 _____ and me,

Say hello to my **2** _____ family.

2 **Look and write.**

> baby   dad   mom

_____

Family 1

_____

_____

Family 2

3 **Look at 2 and complete.**

MATH ZONE

Family 1   There are ☐ people.

Family 2   There are ☐ people.

1 Which family is big?
Family _____ is
_____ .

2 Which family is small?
_____

Welcome to my family

I will learn family words.

1 Complete the family words.

ad   by   cle   ~~ma~~   nt   om   pa   sin   ter   ther

1 grand___ma___   2 d_____   3 bro_____   4 grand_____

5 m_____   6 ba_____   7 sis_____   8 un_____

9 au_____   10 cou_____

2 Look and write.

1 __grandma__

2 _____

3 _____

4 _____

5 _____

6 _____

7 _____

8 _____

9 _____

10 _____

3 🔊 💬 Look, listen, and match. Then count and say.

1 triplets   2 only child   3 twins

How many children are there?

There are three brothers. They're triplets.

I can use family words.

Language lab 1

GRAMMAR 1: THIS IS MY / YOUR / HIS / HER

*I will introduce my family using **This is**.*

1 Follow and complete.

 1 ___This___ is me.

 This is _____ soccer ball.

 2 This _____ my brother.

 This is ___my___ teddy bear.

 3 This is _____ sister.

 This is _____ train.

2 Draw you and your partner with toys. Then complete.

This is me. This is _____ .

This is you. This is _____ .

3 Make family bookmarks. Tell your partner.

grandma

This is your grandma!

Yes! This is my grandma. This is her bookmark.

I can introduce my family using This is .

Story lab

READING

I will read a story about family.

My **BIG** family

1 ⚙ Make your story book. → page 101

1 Order and write the page numbers.

2 Complete the story.

3 Draw a cover.

4 Complete the story review.

2 Look and circle Alexander's family. Then write about them.

1 This is _____ _____ , Sara.

2 This _____ _____ mom.

3 This is _____ _____ .

3 ⚙ Draw a party at your house. Then say.

This is my aunt.

I can read a story about family.

1  Look, listen, and write g or k.

Color me !

1 ____ing   2 ____ite   3 ____irl   4 ____ame

2 Complete with the words in 1. Then say.

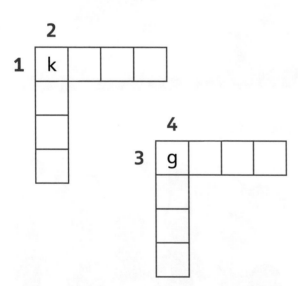

1 | k | | |

3  Listen and write the missing letters. Then say.

1 The ____irl has a ____ite.

2 The ____ing plays a ____ame.

3 The ____irl likes the ____ing.

4 Look, draw, and write.

_____

 use the **g** and **k** sounds.

Experiment lab

MATH: SHAPES

I will learn about shapes.

1 How many sides? Count.

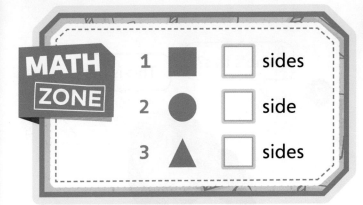

MATH ZONE

1 ▪ ☐ sides

2 ● ☐ side

3 ▲ ☐ sides

2 Color the picture. Then count the shapes and say.

EXPERIMENT TIME

Report

1 Complete the chart.

My jigsaw	
Family	Shapes

2 Write your report.

My family jigsaw

This is my mom, my dad, and me.

There are four triangles in my jigsaw.

My family jigsaw

This is _____.

There are _____

in my jigsaw.

I know about shapes.

Language lab 2

GRAMMAR 2: WHO …?

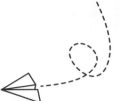

I will ask about family using **Who's this?**

1 ⚙ Ask and answer. Then color and check.

Who's this?

This is his …

1

Who's this?

This is her …

2

2 Look and complete.

1 Who's this?　　　　＿＿＿＿＿＿ his mom.

2 ＿＿＿＿＿ this?　　This is ＿＿＿＿＿＿ .

3 Who's ＿＿＿＿＿ ?　　This ＿＿＿＿＿＿ .

3 💬 Play *Reveal.*

Who's this?

This is your brother!

I can ask about family using Who's this?

Making new friends

COMMUNICATION

> I will introduce my friends.

1 Listen and number.

Nuan

Amin

Samira

2 Read and circle the differences. Then act out.

1
Hello! I'm Samantha.

Hi! I'm Oliver.

2
Pleased to meet you, Oliver.

Nice to meet you, Samantha.

CODE CRACKER

Hi! I'm Leo.

Hello! I'm Ana.

Nice to meet you, Ana.

Pleased to meet you, Leo.

3 Draw finger friends. Role-play making new friends.

Hello! I'm Hugo. Who are you?

Hi! I'm Charlotte. This is my friend Ayesha.

Pleased to meet you, Hugo.

I can introduce my friends.

Create a family play house decoration

Project report

1 Complete for your decoration. Write your family members and color.

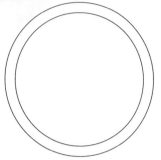  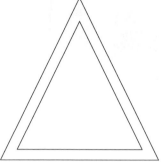

_____ _____ _____

2 Complete your project report.

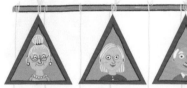

My grandma Rosa   My grandma Ana   My grandpa Carlos

My mom   My dad   My aunt Tania   My uncle Ricardo

My brother Diego   Me   Baby Andrea

My family play house decoration

This is my family play house decoration.
Look! There's a triangle. This is my grandma, Rosa.
There's a square. This is my mom.
There's a circle. This is my brother, Diego.

My family play house decoration

This is my family play house decoration.
Look! There's a _____.
This is my _____.
There's a _____.
This _____.

I can make a family decoration.

3 Present your report to your family and friends.

This is my family decoration. There are three triangles. This is my grandma, Rosa.

4 Look and circle Ana's family.

1 mom / uncle   2 baby / aunt

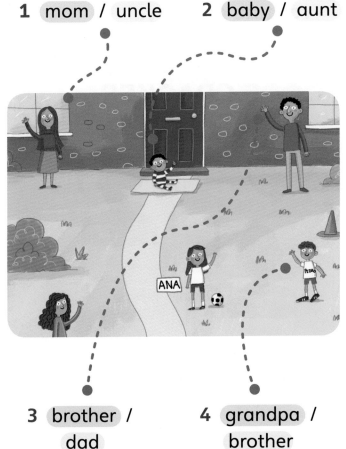

3 brother / dad   4 grandpa / brother

5 Look at 4. Ask and answer.

Who's this?

This is her mom.

6 Read and complete.

You: Hello! I'm _____ .

Ana: Hi! I'm Ana. Pleased to _____ you.

You: _____ to meet you, too, Ana.

Ana: _____ this?

You: _____ is my friend, _____ .

Ana: Hello, _____ .

4 Puppet show!

⮑ **How can I do a puppet show?**

1 🎧 023 **Listen to the song. Order the actions.**

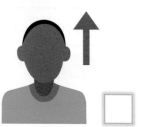 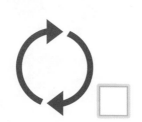  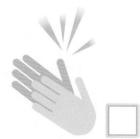

2 Look and write.

hands   head   leg

1 _____

2 _____

3 _____

3 Look and do the actions. Then draw your own routine and say.

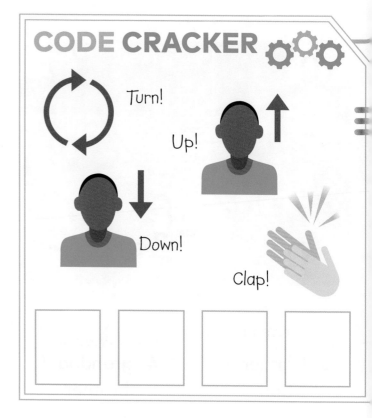

CODE CRACKER

Turn!

Up!

Down!

Clap!

My body

VOCABULARY

I will learn body words.

1 Complete the crossword.

arms   ears   eyes   face   feet   hair
hands   head   legs   mouth   nose

2 Circle and say the face words in 1.

EXTRA VOCABULARY

3 Listen, point, and count. Then play *How many fingers?*

1 ☐ toes 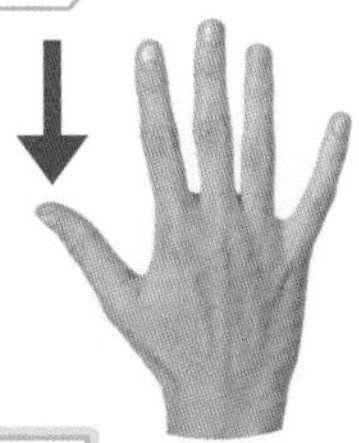   2 ☐ thumb    3 ☐ fingers

Five fingers!

Seven fingers!

How many fingers are there?

There are seven fingers! I win.

CODE CRACKER

I can use body words.

41

Language lab 1

GRAMMAR 1: I / YOU HAVE AND HE / SHE HAS

I will describe people using **have / has.**

1 Read and write **have** or **has.**

1 I _____ brown hair.

2 He _____ blue eyes.

3 You _____ green eyes.

4 She _____ black hair.

2 Read and write the name.

Ed

Olivia

Jilly

Leo

1 She has eight legs. _____

2 He has blue ears. _____

3 He has a brown nose. _____

4 She has orange hair. _____

3 Describe a toy to your partner.

This is my teddy bear. He has two brown ears.

4 Write sentences.

1 I / two / ears

I _have two ears_____.

2 He / two / legs

He has _____.

3 She / one / nose

She _____.

4 You / two / hands

You _____.

I can describe people using have / has .

Story lab

READING

I will read a story about a monster.

It's a monster!

1 🔧 Make your story book. ➡ page 103

1 Order and write the page numbers.

2 Complete the story.

3 Draw a cover and what happens next.

4 Complete the story review.

2 Write about the shadow.

1 It _____ big ears.

2 It has six _____ .

3 It _____ three _____ .

3 🔧 Make a shadow monster. Describe it to your partner.

It has a big mouth.

Phonics lab

I will learn the **z** and **s** sounds.

1 Color **z** red **and** **s** blue.

Color me !

Z S Z S S Z S Z S

2  Listen and circle. Then say.

The sad (zebra) / sister sits in the (zoo) / sun .

3 Write **z** or **s** and say.

1 ____un

2 ____oo

3 ____ing

4 ____ebra

I can use the **z** and **s** sounds.

Experiment lab

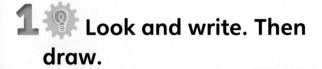

I will learn about the five senses.

1 ✦ Look and write. Then draw.

hear   see   smell   taste   touch

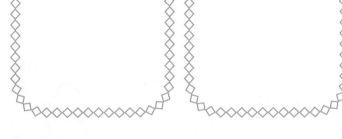

1 I _____ with my hands.

2 I _____ with my mouth.

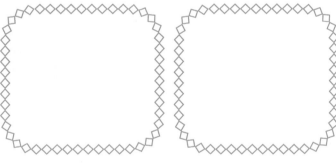

3 I _____ with my eyes.

4 I _____ with my nose.

5 I _____ with my ears.

I know about the five senses.

EXPERIMENT TIME

Report

1 Complete the chart.

Can I guess the taste?		
	My guess	**Result**
Food 1		
Food 2		

2 Write your report.

Can I guess the taste?

Food 1

My guess: It's chocolate.

Result: Yes! It's chocolate!

Can I guess the taste?

Food 1

My guess: It's _____ .

Result: Yes / No

It's _____ .

Food 2

My guess: _____

Result: Yes / No

_____

45

Language lab 2

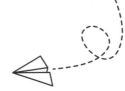

I will describe height using **I'm / You're / He's / She's.**

1 Look and write.

1 I am = ___I'm___

2 You are = _____

3 He is = _____

4 She is = _____

2 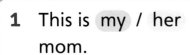 Look, read, and circle.

1 This is my / her mom.

He's / She's tall.

I'm / You're short.

2 This is my / your brother.

He's / She's tall.

I'm / You're short.

3 026 Listen and write. Then measure and write about you and your partner.

CODE CRACKER

1 [l] . [2] meters tall

2 [ ] . [ ] meters tall

3 [ ] . [ ] meters tall

4 [ ] . [ ] meters tall

I'm [ ] . [ ] meters tall.

My partner is [ ] . [ ] meters tall.

What a big teddy bear!

COMMUNICATION

I will talk about surprising things.

1 Look, listen, and write.

big   small   short   tall

1   What a _____ boat!   2   What a _____ boat!

3   What a _____ girl!   4   What a _____ girl!

2 Use and to complete the sentences. Then use and to describe your partner.

You're tall and you have black hair.

CODE CRACKER

1   He's short. His dad is tall.

   He's short ___and his dad___
   _____ .

2   She's short. Her sister is tall.

   She's short _____
   _____ .

I can talk about surprising things.

Create a puppet show

Project report

1 Complete for your puppet and your partner's puppet.

	My puppet	My partner's puppet
Name		
Size		
Body parts		

2 Complete your project report.

My puppet
This is my puppet. Her name is Big Bug.
She has three eyes. She has six legs.
She's small.

Our puppet show

This is my puppet. _____

name is _____ . _____

has _____ _____ and she's /

he's _____ .

This is my partner's puppet. _____

name is _____ . _____ has

_____ _____ and she's /

he's _____ .

I can do a puppet show.

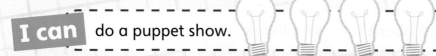

3  **Present your report to your family and friends.**

> This is my puppet. Her name is Big Bug. She has a green face!

4 Look, read, and write the name.

 Uncle Bob    Mrs. Bag    Pinocchio    Aunt Moo    Ribbit    Mary-Jo

1 He has a big nose. _____

2 She has small feet. _____

3 He has big eyes. _____

4 She's small. _____

5 She has a small, green nose. _____

6 He has a big, red mouth _____

5  **Look at 4. Point and tell your partner something surprising.**

> What big eyes!

6 Read and complete. Then write a clue for your partner.

He has two eyes.
He has a red mouth.
He has small hands.
He's big.
His name is _____ .

He / She has _____ .
He / She has _____ .
He / She has _____ .
He's / She's _____ .
His / Her name is _____ .

Now go to your Progress Chart on page 2.

2 Checkpoint

1 Circle the odd one out.

1 mom   aunt   cousin   face
2 arms   nose   feet   uncle
3 short   grandpa   tall   big
4 grandma   baby   sister   tall

2 Draw a path and color.

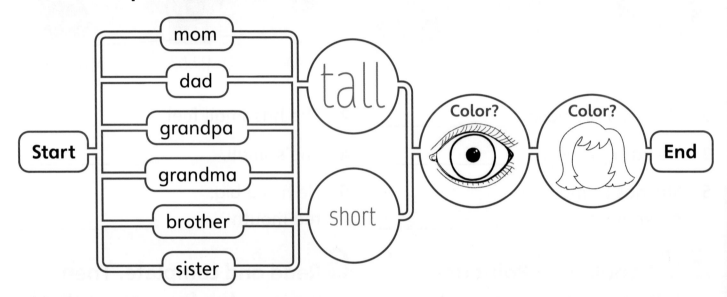

Start   mom   dad   grandpa   grandma   brother   sister   tall   short   Color?   Color?   End

3 Look at 2. Complete and draw.

1 Who's this?

This is _____ _____ .

2 Tall or short?

He / She is _____ .

3 Eye color?

He / She has _____ _____ .

4 Hair color?

He / She has _____ _____ .

Let's celebrate

1 Look and color.

1 red	2 pink
3 blue	4 purple
5 green	6 orange
7 yellow	

2 Read and complete.

brother   China   dragon   hair   head   lantern

1 This is New Year in _____ .

2 This is her _____ . He has black _____ .

3 This is a red _____ .

4 This is a Chinese _____ . It has a yellow and green _____ .

3 Play *Guess the New Year Festival.*

There are tall puppets.

It's New Year in Ecuador!

Yes!

51

5 The perfect pet

How can we choose the perfect class pet?

1 028 **Listen to the song. Then match.**

1 Woof! •

2 Clip clop! •

3 Croak! •

• horse

• frog

• dog

2 **Look and complete.**

1 What's this?

It's a _____ .

2 What's this?

It's _____ .

3 What's this?

_____

3 **Read and cross ☒ the false sentences.**

CODE CRACKER

1

It's small. ☐

It has four eyes. ☐

It has four legs. ☐

It's yellow. ☐

2

It's small. ☐

It has two ears. ☐

It has three legs. ☐

It's brown. ☐

Animals around us

VOCABULARY

I will learn pet words.

1 Complete the puzzle. There are two extra words.

bird   cat   dog   fish   frog   hamster   horse   lizard   mouse   rabbit

1
2
3
4
5
6
7
8

Mystery animal: _____

2 Look at 1. Write the two missing animals.

_____   _____

EXTRA VOCABULARY

3 029 Look, listen, and number. Then ask and answer.

It has eight legs. It's black and brown.

It's a spider!

☐ spider   ☐ tortoise   ☐ stick insect

I can use pet words.

Language lab 1

GRAMMAR 1: I / YOU / HE / SHE CAN / CAN'T

*I will talk about actions using **can** and **can't**.*

1 Read and complete. Then match.

> but   can   can't   It   it   swim

1   He can run, _____ he _____ fly. •

2   It _____ swim, but _____ can't hop. •

3   _____ can fly, but it can't _____ . •

2 🗨 Talk to your partner. Check ☑ or cross ☒.

CODE CRACKER ⚙⚙⚙

hop	clap	swim	sing	climb	fly

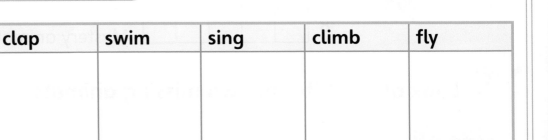

I can hop, but I can't fly!

OK. You can hop, but you can't fly.

3 Write about your partner. Use the information in 2.

He / She / can / can't _____ , but _____ .

_____

 **I can** talk about actions using can and can't .

Story lab

I will read a story about a hat.

My hat can hop!

1 Make your story book. ➡ **page 105**

1 Order and write the page numbers.

2 Complete the story.

3 Draw a cover.

4 Complete the story review.

2 **Read and match. There is one extra sentence.**

My hat can fly! ●

It can hop! ●

Look! It's a horse! ●

Sara, your hat can swim! ●

Look! It can climb! ●

3 **Write about the frog in the story.**

The frog _____ green.

It has _____ legs.

It can _____ , but it can't _____ .

It can _____ , but _____ .

 read a story about a hat.

Phonics lab

*I will learn the **m** and **n** sounds.*

1 Look, listen, and write m or n.

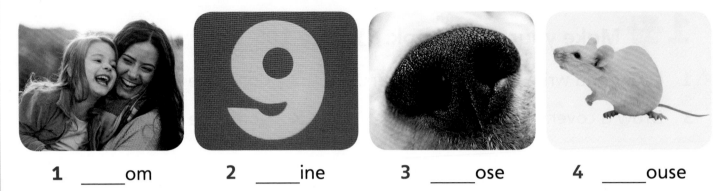

1 _____om   2 _____ine   3 _____ose   4 _____ouse

2 Help the mouse find the nut. Follow and say m or n.

3 Write the missing letters.

_____y _____ame's Nancy. What's your _____ame?

_____y _____ame's Mark.

4 Look at 3. Ask and answer with your own names.

I can use the **m** and **n** sounds.

Experiment lab

I will learn about animal and plant needs.

1 ⚙ What does a cat need to live? Check ☑ and say.

1

2

3

4

5

EXPERIMENT TIME

Report

1 Circle the materials you used. Then color the correct flower.

white flower   red flower   pot
insects   water   food dye

Step 1

Step 2

2 Write your report.

Equipment	Results
white flower	Step 1: The flower is white.
pot	Step 2: The flower drinks the water and food dye. The flower is red.
water	
food dye	

Equipment	Results
_____	Step 1: The water is red. The flower is _____ .
_____	Step 2: The flower drinks the _____ and food dye.
_____	
_____	_____

I know about animal and plant needs.

Language lab 2

GRAMMAR 2: WE CAN / THEY CAN'T

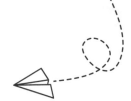

I will describe actions using **We can / They can't.**

1 Look and write T (True) or F (False).

1 Ed and Rosie can't swim quickly. ☐

2 Zara and Dennis can swim quickly. ☐

3 Mark and Eva can run slowly. ☐

4 Sunil and Maisie can't run slowly. ☐

2 Correct the false sentences in 1.

1 _____ 2 _____

3  Have a relay race.

MATH ZONE

1 Play in four groups.

2 Groups run and hop for five meters.

3 Complete the chart.

	Group 1 time	Group 2 time	Group 3 time	Group 4 time
run				
hop				

We can't run quickly, but Group 2 can run quickly.

4 Talk about the results.

4 Write about your relay race in 3.

Group 1 can run quickly. _____ _____

  describe actions using We can / They can't .

My favorite animal

COMMUNICATION

 I will describe my favorite animal.

1 🎧 031 Look, listen, and write.

> Ava   Ben   Ethan   Mia

1 _____ 2 _____ 3 _____ 4 _____

2 💬 Play *Guess who*. Use the children in 1.

Her favorite animal is a bird.

It's Ava!

Yes!

3 💡 Play *Draw and guess*.

It's small. It has two legs. It can fly ...

Your favorite animal is a bird!

Yes! My favorite animal is a bird.

I can describe my favorite animal.

Choose the perfect class pet

Project report

1 Complete for your perfect class pet.

Our perfect class pet	
Is it big or small?	
What can it do?	
What does it eat?	

2 Complete your project report.

Our perfect class pet
Our perfect class pet is a rabbit. Its name is Hoppy. It can hop quickly. It's small and white. It eats plants and drinks water.

Our perfect class pet

Our perfect class pet is
a _____.
Its name is _____.
It can _____
_____.
It's _____.
It eats _____ and
drinks _____.

3 Present your report to your family and friends.

This is our perfect class pet. Its name is Hoppy. It can hop quickly!

I can choose the perfect class pet.

4 Read, look, and write. There are two extra animals.

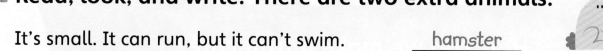

1 It's small. It can run, but it can't swim. _____hamster_____

2 It can fly and it has two legs. _____

3 It can hop and it has big eyes. _____

4 It can hop and it can run quickly. _____

5 It can swim, but it can't fly. _____

6 It's small. It has four legs and big ears. _____

7 It eats insects. It can climb, but it can't hop. _____

8 It has four legs. It eats fish. _____

rabbit

lizard

hamster

horse

frog   mouse   fish   bird   cat   dog

5 🗨 Look at 4. Choose your favorite animal.

My favorite animal is the hamster.

6 Read and complete. Then write a clue for your partner.

It's small and brown.
It has four legs.
It eats plants.
It can run and climb.
It's a _____.

It's _____.
It has _____.
It eats _____.
It can _____.
It's a _____.

6 Fruit bowl!

How can we make a fruit café?

1 🎵 032 Listen to the song. Write the number.

☐ mango   ☐ apples   ☐ oranges

2 Circle the odd one out. Then say.

3 Look at 2 and answer.

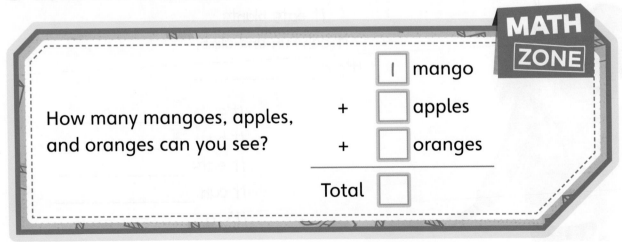

MATH ZONE

How many mangoes, apples, and oranges can you see?

1	mango
+	☐ apples
+	☐ oranges
Total	☐

Lots of fruit

VOCABULARY

I will learn fruit words.

1 Look and write.

1  (r a / e n o / g)

2  (w i / i k)

3  (i e / p a e / n l p / p)

4 (e r a / p)

_____   _____   _____   _____

5  (a e / l p p)

6 (a n / n b a / a)

7  (r l e / m t n w o / e a)

_____   _____   _____

2 Match and draw.

5 strawberr ●   ● s

2 mango ●   ● ies

8 grape ●   ● es

EXTRA VOCABULARY

3 🎧 033 Complete. Then listen and repeat.

1   **2**   **3**   **4**   **5**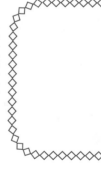

peach   plum   _____   papaya   _____

I can use fruit words.

Language lab 1

GRAMMAR 1: I / WE / THEY LIKE / DON'T LIKE

*I will talk about what **we like** and **don't like**.*

1 Read and match.

1 What do we like? •
2 What do they like? •
3 What do you like? •

• We like pears.
• I like oranges.
• They like mangoes.

2 Read and circle.

1 I like strawberries (and) / but I like watermelon.

2 We like bananas (and) / but we don't like grapes.

3 They don't like pears (and) / but they don't like apples.

4 You like kiwis (and) / but you don't like pineapples.

3 Read and write T (True) or F (False).

1 We like pears and watermelons. ☐

2 They like grapes, but they don't like bananas. ☐

3 We like mangoes, but we don't like pineapples. ☐

4 I don't like oranges, but I like apples. ☐

  I can talk about what (we like) and (don't like).

Story lab

READING

I will read a story about a fruit garden.

1 ⚙ Make your story book. ➡ page 107

1 Order and write the page numbers.

2 Complete the story.

3 Draw a cover.

4 Complete the story review.

2 💬 Check ☑ the fruit Sara and Alexander like. Then ask and answer.

What fruit do they like?

They like oranges, but they don't like kiwis.

3 What's in Grandpa's smoothie? Complete.

A _____ .

A _____ .

An _____ .

I will learn the
l and *r* sounds.

1 🔊 034 Look, listen, and write l or r.

1 ____emon   2 ____abbit   3 ____eaf   4 ____obot

Color me!

2 Look and write the words. Then add more words.

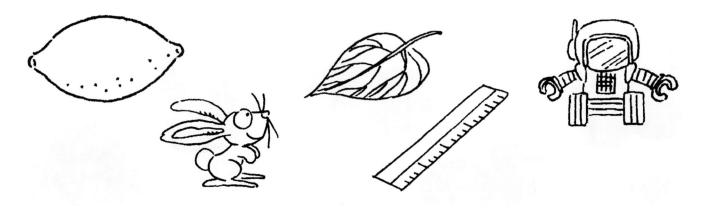

l	r
_____	_____
_____	_____

3 Write the missing letters. Then say.

1 ____ucy has long ____egs.   2 There's a ____abbit on the ____oad.

 I can use the l and r sounds.

Experiment lab

SCIENCE: LIFE CYCLE OF FRUIT

I will learn about the life cycle of fruit.

1 Read and number.

CODE CRACKER

The flowers become fruit.

Trees grow from seeds.

There are seeds in the fruit.

Flowers grow on the tree.

EXPERIMENT TIME

Report

1 Complete the chart.

1 seed	2–5 seeds	6–10 seeds	10+ seeds	Big seeds	Small seeds

2 Write your report.

How do we classify fruit *seeds*?
Results
There is one *seed* in the mango.
It's a big seed.
There are six *seeds* in the apple.
They are small seeds.

How do we classify fruit *seeds*?
Results
There _____
in the _____ .
_____
_____
_____

I know about the life cycle of fruit.

Language lab 2

GRAMMAR 2: HE / SHE LIKES / DOESN'T LIKE

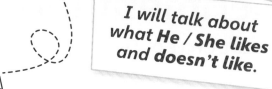

I will talk about what **He / She likes** and **doesn't like**.

1 Look, read, and complete.

1   What _____ Phoebe like?

☺ She _____ kiwis, apples, grapes, strawberries, and oranges.

☹ _____ bananas.

2   What does Simon _____ ?

☺ He _____ kiwis, bananas, grapes, and oranges.

☹ _____ apples and strawberries.

2 Match the children in 1 to the fruit salads. Write Phoebe or Simon.

1 _____

2 _____

3 Follow and write about Tanya and Omar.

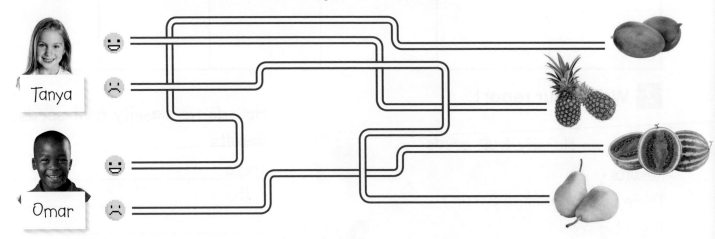

1   Tanya _____ , but she doesn't like _____ .

2   Omar _____ , but he _____ .

I can talk about what he / she likes and doesn't like .

Me too!

COMMUNICATION

I will learn how to agree with my friends.

1 **Listen and draw 😃 or 🙁 .**

Ben and Madison

1  **2**  **3**  **4**  **5**  **6**

2  **Ask and answer about the children in 1.**

Ben and Madison don't like apples.

Me neither!

3 **Play *Surprise box*.**

What is it?

It's a train. I like trains.

Me too!

 agree with my friends.

Make a class fruit café

Project report

1 Complete for your class fruit café.

Our class fruit café	
😃	🙁

2 Complete your project report.

Our class fruit café

In our café, we like kiwi and orange smoothies. We like apple and mango popsicles, too. We don't like fruit salad.

Our class fruit café

In our café, we like

_____ .

We like _____

_____ , too.

_____

3 Present your report to your family and friends.

This is our class fruit café. We like kiwi and orange smoothies!

I can make a fruit café.

4 Read and write T (True) or F (False).

1 He likes bananas, but he doesn't like pears. ☐

2 He likes kiwis, but he doesn't like apples. ☐

3 She likes watermelons, but she doesn't like grapes. ☐

4 She likes strawberries, but she doesn't like mangoes. ☐

5 They like oranges, but they don't like pineapples. ☐

6 They like bananas, but they don't like watermelons. ☐

Jackson

Abigail

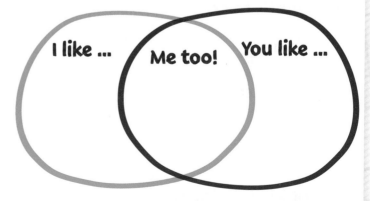

5 Correct the false sentences in 4.

6 Look and complete with your partner.

I like ...   Me too!   You like ...

Now go to your Progress Chart on page 2.

3 Checkpoint
UNITS 5 AND 6

1 Read and complete.

apple   dog   grapes   horse   kiwi   lizard   mango   mouse   orange   rabbit

Pets	
Fruit	

2 Draw a path.

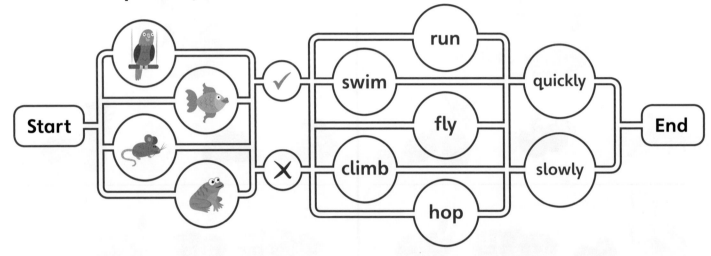

Start — swim — run — quickly — End — fly — climb — slowly — hop

3 Look at 2. Complete and draw.

1   What's this?

It's a _____ .

2   Can or can't?

It _____

_____

quickly / slowly .

4 Look, read, and complete.

Pets

☺ I like _____ .

☹ I don't like _____ .

Fruit

☺ I _____ .

☹ I _____ .

Let's make a snake

1 Read and check ☑ the correct sentences.

1 a The snake can climb quickly, but it can't run. ☐

  b The snake can run quickly, but it can't climb. ☐

2 a The snail can swim quickly, but it can't climb. ☐

  b The snail can climb slowly, but it can't run. ☐

3 a The elephant can climb slowly, but it can't run. ☐

  b The elephant can swim quickly, but it can't climb. ☐

2 Look, match, and write.

> apples   bananas   elephants   mice   snails   snakes

1

_____

2

_____

3

_____

 They like _____.

 They like _____.

 They like _____.

3 Ask and answer.

What do snails like?

Snails like apples.

7 Let's get active

How can we plan an activity day?

1 🎧 Listen to the song. Check ☑ or cross ☒.

036

CODE CRACKER

swim	fly	hop	climb	play music	dance	sing

2 💬 What can you do? Tell your partner.

I can't swim, but I can sing.

3 Look and complete.

1 I can _____ .

2 I can _____ .

3 I can _____ .

I can dance!

VOCABULARY

I will learn hobbies.

1 Find and circle the hobby words.

1 r t d a n c e p

2 w y x s i n g l

3 q d r a w h m i

4 o i p a i n t k

5 y z e s w i m r

6 a e c l i m b o

2 Read and complete with play, read, or ride.

1 _____ a book

2 _____ soccer

3 _____ a bike

4 _____ music

EXTRA VOCABULARY

3  Look, listen, and write. Circle the odd one out.

1 _____ a scooter

2 _____ a horse

3 _____ a board game

I can use hobby words.

Language lab 1

GRAMMAR 1: I / YOU / WE / THEY SWIM / DON'T SWIM

I will ask about hobbies using action words.

1 Order and write.

1   do?   activities   you   What   do

_____

2   but   play   music.   I   don't   I   sing,

_____

3   do   What   do?   activities   they

_____

4   draw,   They   don't   they   but   paint.

_____

2 Ask and answer. Complete the tally chart.

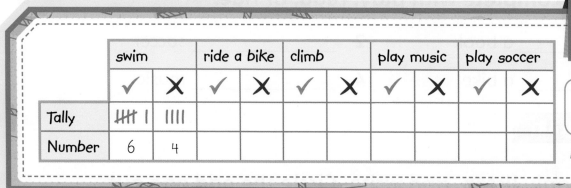

	swim		ride a bike		climb		play music		play soccer	
	✓	✗	✓	✗	✓	✗	✓	✗	✓	✗
Tally	ⵝ I	IIII								
Number	6	4								

MATH ZONE

What activities do you do?

I play soccer, but I don't ride a bike.

3 Look at 2 and complete.

1 _____ students ride a bike, but _____ students don't _____

2 _____ students _____ , but _____ students _____

3 _____ students _____ , _____

I can ask about hobbies using action words.

Story lab

READING

I will read a story about hobbies.

Circus School

1 ⚙ Make your story book. ➡ page 109

1 Order and write the page numbers.

2 Complete the story.

3 Draw a cover.

4 Complete the story review.

2 Read and circle T (True) or F (False).

1 I play soccer in the afternoon.   T / F

2 I dance in the afternoon.   T / F

3 I don't fly in the afternoon.   T / F

4 I don't climb trees in the afternoon.   T / F

3 Correct the false sentences in 2.

I don't _____
       in the afternoon.

I _____ .

4 💡 Look and write.

bike   tricycle   unicycle

_____   _____

_____

I can read a story about hobbies.

Phonics lab

I will learn the **h** and **w** sounds.

1 [038] Look, listen, and circle.

Color me !

1   Harry is (hot / dot / not).

He has a lot of (fair / hair / house).

He is wearing a (bat / hat / cat).

2   (We / He / I) are friends.

We (talk / walk / run).

We like (mangoes / apples / watermelons).

2 [039] Listen and color h words in blue. Color w words in red.

3 Write words beginning with h or w.

h	w
_____	_____
_____	_____
_____	_____
_____	_____

78

I can use the **h** and **w** sounds.

Experiment lab

SCIENCE: LIFE CYCLE OF A FROG

I will learn about the life cycle of a frog.

1 Look, number, and write.

CODE CRACKER

frog   frog spawn   froglet   tadpoles

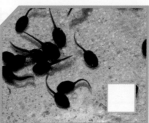

_____   _____   _____   _____

EXPERIMENT TIME

Report

1 Complete the chart.

	Size of tail	Number of legs	Color	Hop	Swim
eggs					
tadpoles					
froglets					
frog					

2 Complete the report.

The life cycle of a frog

1 My frog's eggs can't swim and they can't _____ . They're black.

2 Tadpoles can _____ , but they can't hop. They have a big _____ .

3 _____ can swim, but they can't hop. They have four _____ .

4 _____

I know about the life cycle of a frog.

Language lab 2

GRAMMAR 2: HE / SHE SINGS / DOESN'T SING

> I will ask about actions using **What does …?**

1 Read and match.

1 What activities does he do? •   • She reads, but she doesn't draw.

2 What activities do you do? •   • He sings, but he doesn't swim.

3 What activities does she do? •   • We dance, but we don't climb.

2 Look and complete.

⚽ ✓	🎸 ✗
I _____play soccer_____ .	I _____don't play music_____ .
You _____ .	You _____ .
He _____ .	He _____ .
She _____ .	She _____ .
We _____ .	We _____ .
They _____ .	They _____ .

3 Ask and answer. Then circle and write.

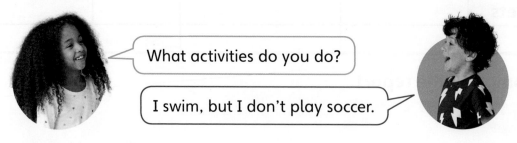

What activities do you do?

I swim, but I don't play soccer.

What does my friend do?

He / She _____ , but he / she doesn't _____ .

He / She _____ , but he / she _____ .

 I can ask about actions using **What does …?**

When are you active?

COMMUNICATION

I will talk about the time of day.

1 📞 040 What does the girl do? Listen and check ☑.

1   2   3

2 💬 Look and follow. Then ask and answer.

Taj

What does Taj do in the morning?

He plays music in the morning.

3 ✳ Make an activity wheel. Then ask and answer.

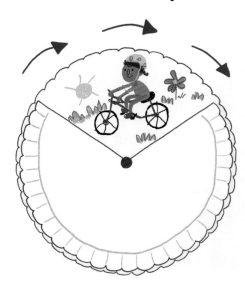

What do you do in the morning?

I ride a bike in the morning.

I can talk about the time of day.

81

PROJECT AND REVIEW UNIT 7

Have an activity day!

1 Check ☑ for your activity day.

dance ☐ read ☐ sing ☐ draw ☐ play soccer ☐ play music ☐

read ☐ paint ☐ climb ☐ swim ☐ run ☐ hop ☐

2 Complete your project report.

Our activity day

At our activity day, we paint, dance, and play music.
We don't play soccer and we don't swim.

Our activity day

At our activity day, we _____

_____

_____ .

We don't _____

_____

_____ .

3 🗨 Present your report to your family and friends.

At our activity day, we paint and dance. We play music, too!

82

I can have an activity day.

4 Read, look, and number.

He climbs at the park. ☐

She rides a bike at the park. ☐

He plays soccer at the park. ☐

She reads at the park. ☐

He plays music at the park. ☐

She draws at the park. ☐

5 Read and write.

bird   fish   frog   lizard

1   It swims, but it doesn't fly.   _____

2   It sings, but it doesn't climb.   _____

3   It hops, but it doesn't run.   _____

4   It climbs, but it doesn't sing.   _____

6 Play *Mime and guess*.

8 Let's dress up

How can I make a weather flap book?

1 Listen to the song. Then write a new verse and sing.

CODE CRACKER

> bag   ball   book   bike

Find your _____ – it's red and blue.

Find your _____ , find your shoes,

Put on your shoes – shoe one, shoe two,

Pick up your _____ and your _____ , too.

2 Look and write.

> feet   hat   head   shoes

1    **2**    **3**    **4**

_____   _____   _____   _____

3 Look and complete.

1

Put on your _____ .

2

Put on your _____ .

3

Put on your _____ .

Colorful clothes

I will learn clothes words.

1 Complete and say the alphabet.

A	B	C	___	E	F	G	H	I	___	K	L	M
■	✖	▬	◗	●	⬠	★	▌	▲	◆	⬡	◢	⬠

N	O	___	Q	R	S	___	U	V	W	X	___	Z
◣	◥	→	↓	←	↑	✚	◇	◗	▶	✹	▢	○

2 Use the code in 1 to write the words.

CODE CRACKER

1 ▌■✚

2 ▬✚■✚

3 ◗←●↑↑

4 ↑▌✚●↑

5 ↑●▲←✚

6 →■◣✚↑

3 🎧 042 Look, listen, and number. Use the code in 1 to write the words.

 ☐ ▬■→

_____

 ☐ ✖✚✚✚↑

_____

 ☐ ↑■◣◗■◢↑

_____

I can use clothes words.

85

Language lab 1

GRAMMAR 1: IN, ON, AND UNDER

I will talk about where clothes are using in, on, and under.

1 Look, read, and complete.

in   on   under

1 The sweater is _____ the bag.

2 The socks are _____ the bag.

3 The sweater is _____ the bag.

2 Look, read, and write.

1 The coat is on _____.

2 The shoes are _____.

3 _____.

4 _____.

3 Play *Remember the room.*

1 Look at the picture for one minute.

2 Cover the picture.

3 Tell your partner about the picture.

The doll is on the chair.

Yes! Well done.

I can say where clothes are using in , on , and under .

Story lab

READING

I will read a story about a pirate party.

Pirate Party

1 Make your story book. ➡ page 111

1 Order and write the page numbers.

2 Complete the story.

3 Draw a cover.

4 Complete the story review.

2 Circle Polly's costume in blue. Circle Sara's costume in red.

3 Read and complete.

> big   coat   hat   pants   small   T-shirt

1 Polly has a _____ skirt.

2 Polly has a small _____ .

3 Polly has a blue and white _____ .

4 Sara has a red _____ .

5 Sara has a _____ hat.

6 Sara has brown _____ .

 I can read a story about a pirate party.

*I will learn the **v** and **f** sounds.*

1 **Color v blue and f red. Then say.**

Color me !

2 **Look, listen, and write the missing letters.**

1  The ____ish has a ____lower.

2  The ____ox has ____our ____eet.

3  The ____et has a ____an.

3 **Find and circle the words.**

o	k	f	e	v	a
f	l	o	w	e	r
i	m	x	p	t	s
s	z	i	d	y	u
h	b	v	a	n	g

I can use the **v** and **f** sounds.

Experiment lab

SCIENCE: THE WEATHER FORECAST

I will learn about the weather.

1 Look, read, and complete.

snowy   sunny   windy

🌐 WEATHER FORECAST

In the morning	In the afternoon	In the evening

1 In the morning, it's _____ .

2 In the afternoon, it's _____ .

3 In the evening, it's _____ .

EXPERIMENT TIME

Report

1 Check ☑ the weather today.

 ☐   ☐   ☐  ☐   ☐  ☐

very windy ☐   windy ☐   not very windy ☐   not windy ☐

2 Complete your report.

The weather today

It's rainy and it's cold.
My windsock moves slowly.
It's not very windy.

The weather today

It's _____ and it's _____ .
My windsock _____ .

_____

I know about the weather.

Language lab 2

GRAMMAR 2: WHERE IS / WHERE ARE ...?

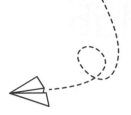

I can ask where clothes are using **Where ...?**

1 Read and circle.

1 Where (is) / are my umbrella? It (is) / are in your bag.

2 Where is / (are) my gloves? They is / (are) under the chair.

3 Where (is) / are your cap? (It) / They is on your head!

4 Where is / (are) your boots? It / (They) are in the car.

2 Read the questions and answers in 1. Then look and match.

3 Write questions. Then hide items for your partner to find.

My scavenger hunt

Where are the crayons? Where is the ball?

_____

_____

_____

_____

Where is the ball?

It's in the hat!

I can ask where clothes are using Where ...?

What's the weather like?

COMMUNICATION

I will ask and answer about the weather.

1 🎧 044 Look, listen, and number.

2 ⚙ Make weather cards. Play *Snap!*

rainy

What's the weather like?

It's rainy!

Snap!

3 Look, read, and circle. Then complete for today and say.

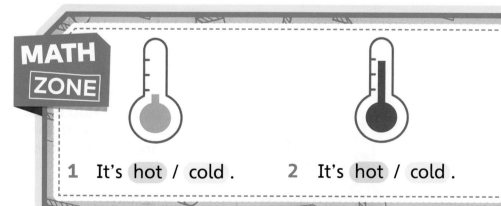

MATH ZONE

1 It's (hot / cold).   2 It's (hot / cold).   3 It's _____ .

What's the weather like today?   It's hot.

I can ask and answer about the weather.

Make a weather flap book

Project report

1 Complete the chart for your flap book.

	Weather 1: _____	Weather 2: _____
Clothes		

2 Complete your project report.

My weather flap book

It's hot. She has shorts, a cap, and a T-shirt. She has socks and shoes, too.

cap

T-shirt
shorts
socks
shoes

My weather flap book

_____
_____
_____
_____
_____
_____

3 Present your report to your family and friends.

This is my weather flap book. It's hot. She has shorts! She has a cap and a T-shirt, too!

I can make a weather flap book.

4 Look, read, and check ☑ the correct sentences.

1 a The ball is in the bag. ☐

  b The ball is under the bag. ☐

2 a The pencil case is on the purple book. ☐

  b The pencil case is under the pencil sharpener. ☐

3 a The hat is under the car. ☐

  b The hat is in the car. ☐

4 a The boy is on the book. ☐

  b The boy is under the book. ☐

5 Look at 4. Read and answer.

1 Where are the green shoes? _____

2 Where is the purple book? _____

3 Where is the black and white bag? _____

4 Where is the book? _____

6 Play *Hot or cold*.

Where is your book?

Cold … cold … hot!

It's under your sweater!

Yes!

4 Checkpoint

1 Look and sort. Circle the words in the correct color.

read   draw   on   dress   coat   cloudy

in

under   hot

cold

paint   sing   shorts   skirt   rainy

2 Draw a path.

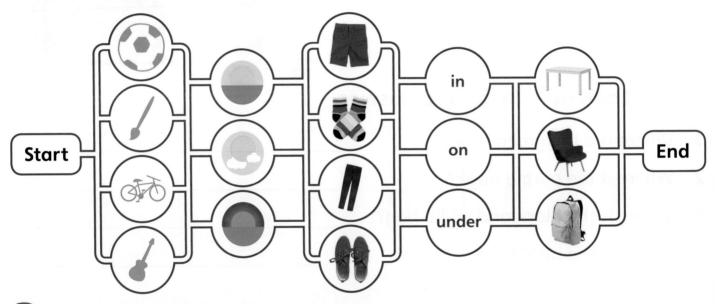

Start   in   End

on

under

3 Look at 2. Complete and draw.

1   What activities does he / she do?

He / She _____ .

2   When?

In the _____ .

3   Where are the clothes?

The _____ are in /
on / under the _____ .

Entertainment

1 Circle the Bollywood costumes in **red**.
Circle the Broadway costumes in **blue**.

2 Find and write the words. Then look at **1** and complete.

black   green   red   green

1   The Bollywood _____ is _____ .

2   The _____ is _____ and _____ .

3   The tap _____ are _____ .

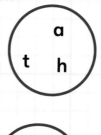
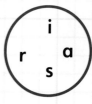

3 Play *Guess the show.*

There are green hats.

Yes!

It's Bollywood.

OUR WORLD

INTRO:

Here we stand: children of every age,
This is our world and the world's our stage.
We can laugh, we can cry — we can float, we can fly,
We can dance, we can sing — we can do almost anything
in OUR world ... our *beautiful* world.

VERSE 1:

Some of us are small; some of us are tall,
Some of us are shy; some say hi to everybody,
Some of us like numbers; some of us love words,
Some of us watch football, and some of us watch the birds!

(CHORUS)

This is our world ... we're different but the same.
We live and learn together — we get to know each other ...
in OUR world ... our *beautiful* world.

VERSE 2:

Some of us like music; some of us like cars,
Some of us draw pictures, looking at the stars,
Some of us are scientists, trying to find the code,
All of us can help a friend and give a hand to hold.

This is our world — there's room for everyone.
We learn to live together, and we have a lot of fun ...
In **our** world ... in **our** world ... in our beautiful world!

Unit 1

A story about toys.

Let's play together

It's an airplane!

It's _____!

It's a bus!

No, no, no. It's _____!

Hello! What's _____?

It's an airplane, a bus, *and* a boat!

Hello! I'm Sara. _____ Polly.

I'm Lee.

Hi! I'm Alexander. Let's play!

Hi! _____ Lily.

Characters

Lily

Lee

Sara

Alexander

Polly

My favorite character:

_____

My favorite story picture: ☐

☆ ☆ ☆

No, no, no.
It's _____ !

No, no, no. _____
a boat!

What's this?

It's a _____ .
Here.

_____ play together.

Unit 2

A **story** about a play house.

A **rainbow** play house

Polly!

Look! Now _____ green paint!

The play house is _____ . Let's decorate it.

Good idea!

There are _____ and a glue stick.

Look at the _____ play house!

Well done, Polly!

_____ this?

_____ a play house.

Come in!

Characters

Lily

Lee

Sara

Alexander

Polly

My favorite character:

_____

My favorite story picture: ☐

What's _____ ?

It's a rainbow.

There are yellow, blue, and red _____ .

Watch out, Polly!

Wow! There _____ toys and books.

TOYS

There's orange paint and purple _____ , too.

Unit 3

A **STORY** about a family.

My **BIG** family

Characters

Lily

Lee

Sara

Alexander

Sofia

This is Lily and _____ Lee.

Nice to meet you!

Come to the party!

I know ... let's have a party in the _____ !

This is my grandpa.

_____ !

Nice to meet you. Please sit down.

101

Unit 4

A story about a monster.

It's a monster!

Stop! It's your _____ !

And it's your cousin Sofia and _____ teddy bear!

Look!

What a big shadow!

What happens next?
Read and draw.

Let's play with the toys!

Good idea.

_____ ?

This is my doll. Hello!

Characters

Lily

Lee

Sara

Alexander

Sofia

Uncle

My favorite character:

_____

My favorite story picture: ☐

☆ ☆ ☆

It _____ three heads!

_____ has six arms!

It has big ears!

Help! _____ a monster!

This is _____.
Nice to meet you!

Shh! Listen!

Hello! _____ I play?

_____, Sofia!

What a big _____!

104

Unit 5

A story about a hat.

My hat can hop!

Look! It's a _____ !

Sara, _____ hat can swim!

My _____ animal is a bird.

_____ favorite animal is a _____ . Bye, Frog!

Look at _____ hat!

_____ can hop!

Characters

Lily

Lee

Sara

Alexander

Polly

My favorite character:

_____

My favorite story picture: ☐

☆ ☆ ☆

_____ a magic hat!

Watch out, Polly! You _____ swim!

My hat can fly!

Come on!

Look! It can _____!

My hat _____ hop, climb, or swim ...

... the frog *can* hop, climb, and swim!

And Polly can fly!

106

Unit 6

A story about a fruit garden.

Bird food

Now I have a mango, _____ banana, and _____ orange.

Look!

I _____ pineapples.

_____ , but look … I have four bananas!

Here – a banana, _____ , and orange smoothie for you. And a _____ salad for the birds!

Mmm! It's delicious. _____ !

This is my garden. _____ fruit do you like?

Let's make fruit _____ !

We like oranges and mangoes, _____ we don't like kiwis.

Characters

 Grandpa

 Sara

 Alexander

 Polly

My favorite character:

_____

My favorite story picture: ☐

Mmm, I _____ bananas!

Sara! Now _____ have three bananas.

_____ make smoothies!

_____ out!

I _____ oranges.

_____ . Look, I have six oranges and two mangoes.

Look at Polly and her friends! _____ don't like bird food …

… but _____ like fruit!

Unit 7

A story about hobbies.

Circus School

I _____ through the air!

Wow! I _____ circus school.

_____ don't climb trees and you _____ play soccer. What activities _____ you do?

I go to _____ school!

This is _____ teacher, Mr. Chuckles.

Welcome to Circus _____!

_____, Mr. Chuckles!

Let's _____!

_____, I don't play soccer in the _____.

Characters

Alexander

Sara

Lee

Lily

Mr. Chuckles

My favorite character:

_____

My favorite story picture: ☐

Look! I _____ climb!

Wow! You can climb _____, Lee!

Look! I _____, too!

You're _____!

Let's _____ trees!

No, _____ don't climb _____ in the afternoon.

I _____ a unicycle!

Watch out!

Unit 8

A story about a pirate party.

Pirate Party

Sara, your _____ is small!

Your _____ is small!

And your _____ is small!

The skirt is _____ the _____ .

Thank you!

Now we _____ all ready. Let's go to the _____ !

Wait, Sara! Tie _____ shoelaces!

It's _____ pirate party _____ !

I like your pirate _____ , Lily. My pirate clothes are in my _____ .

Characters

Alexander · Sara · Lee · Lily · Polly

My favorite character:

_____

My favorite story picture: ☐

☆ ☆ ☆

The T-shirt is _____ the _____ .

Thank you!

The hat is _____ the _____ .

_____ you!

Look at your _____ , Sara! Watch out!

Ahh! _____ bag!

This _____ my costume.
This _____ Polly's costume!
My _____ is in my bag.

Unit 1

Creativity Critical Thinking Coding  Communication

Unit 2

Creativity Critical Thinking  Coding Communication

Unit 3

Creativity Critical Thinking Coding   Communication

Unit 4

Creativity Critical Thinking Coding   Communication

Unit 5

Creativity

Critical Thinking

Coding

Communication

Unit 6

Creativity

Critical Thinking

Coding

Communication

Unit 7

Creativity

Critical Thinking

Coding

Communication

Unit 8

Creativity

Critical Thinking

Coding

Communication